How
NATIONAL LOTTERY

A Desperate Approach

IDEAS UNLIMITED (PUBLISHING)

Published by:
Ideas Unlimited (Publishing)
P.O. Box 125, Portsmouth
Hampshire PO1 4PP

© 1994 Ideas Unlimited (Publishing)

ISBN: 1 871964 14 8

Printed & Bound in Great Britain.

This book is dedicated to
the first jackpot winner of the
UK National Lotteries.

GOOD LUCK!!

ACKNOWLEDGMENTS

First and foremost I would like to convey my sincere gratitude to Mrs Muriel Wykes for giving us permission to use works from her late husband's excellent book entitled "Gambling". The author of this book, Mr Alan Wykes used his unquestionable style, extensive research and that care, sensitivity and wit which only a few authors can tap into to produce the masterpiece which is without a doubt THE authority on the subject of Gambling.

I would like to thank Liz Garrad who took on the very difficult task of researching and writing about the thoughts and actions of the ordinary person in the street, from the point when they buy a lottery ticket to the actual scenario of winning the jackpot. Her findings have been written with her own exquisite style and wit.

My sincere gratitude also goes to Terry McKenna Professor of Mathematics for his contribution in working out the odds of winning the National Lottery and presenting them in comparison with other odds which are more readily understood.

ACKNOWLEDGMENTS

Once again our talented cartoonist, Willy Sanker, has done his work in bringing the text of the book to life with his own brand of humour, through a set of artistically drawn cartoons.

I thank the "Standard Press Analysts Ltd" of London SE1 for the professional and helpful manner in which they compiled a complete set of all Newspaper cuttings on the subject of The National Lottery. Their excellent work has made our research a much easier task.

I also thank Graphic News for allowing us to use their illustration "Who wants to be a millionaire?" which helps to show at a quick glance how The National Lottery will actually work.

Last but no means least, I would like to thank Camelot for providing us with press information on their companies and the workings of The National Lottery. It is a horrendous task and we wish them luck.

CONTENTS

INTRODUCTION

The launch of the National Lottery in November 1994 will create the first National Lottery in the UK for 150 years. It will be the largest single consumer product in the UK, and very soon the largest lottery in the world. It will enable five good causes; Sports, Arts, National Heritage, Charities and Millennium Fund to benefit from a major new source of funding, as well as providing a unique national leisure opportunity.

There will be a new millionaire created almost every week. Who in their right mind is going to pass up the chance of winning a million pounds???? and for those of you who are about to say "It'd wouldn't change my life", well buddy, pardon me, but if a million pounds is not going to change your miserable existence then my advice is - GIVE IT TO ME!!!!! - because it will sure as hell change mine. Though there have been cases where this statement has in fact been true. Many men spend their whole lives lying around the place and being waited on hand and foot - in which case, it's true, your lifestyle won't change an awful lot, just the people who wait on you.

Money may not be able to buy you happiness but it makes being miserable a whole lot more fun!!!

THE HISTORY OF THE LOTTERIES

Lotteries as we think of them today – that is, an organised gamble in which prizes are distributed to lucky ticket holders – didn't burst into the news until Roman times. But in its magical sense it goes back a lot further.

The choosing of a person in relation to some particular task or ceremony has been decided by lot since the earliest civilisation. Some aborigines determine who among them may be causing unrest by throwing a bone into the middle of a circle around which the tribe is gathered. The one to whom the bone points gets the sorcerer's attention and dies within a few days. Even the bushmen of the Kalahari, of whom only a few thousand survive (still living in their own enduring corner of the Stone Age), decide the tribe's daily huntsman by casting a stone. And in the Aztec civilisation in Mexico, the lottery method was often used to decide which of a number of prisoners of war should be taken as the day's sacrifice to the sun god.

HISTORY OF THE LOTTERIES

Lotteries involving the placing of stakes (as distinct from those explained on the previous page) are not very old. The Romans had a form of lottery that required no stakes, but this was virtually a distribution of free gifts given by rich emperors.

1466: The first recorded lottery to involve the buying of tickets and the distribution of prize money was held in Bruges, Belgium on February 24, 1466. It was organised by the widow of the Flemish painter Jan Van Eyck in order to raise money for the poor of the town..

1520: Europe's next lottery didn't appear until 1520, when King Francis I of France legalised the lotteries. Merchants began to organise public lotteries whenever they had some especially valuable product to dispose of , in this way profits were higher than that which would be attained from one individual.

HISTORY OF THE LOTTERIES

1528: Throughout 16th Century Europe private and public lotteries soon got a strong grip on the people. The governments also recognising the potential revenue which could be made for the state, encouraged the idea further. The Lottery fever raged so strongly, particularly in Italy, that in 1528, Lotto de Firenze emerged as the first state run lottery. In Genoa a few years later the admiral statesman Andrea Doria persuaded the government to approve a law providing for the selection of five names from the 120 members of the Genoese nobility for election to the senate. The twice-yearly drawing of the five names aroused interest among the public, and soon betting became an important side issue of the draw. Half of all the money staked was given to the bettors who had guessed the five names correctly; the remainder was kept by the organiser of the game. Some years later the number of names was reduced to 90, and eventually numbers were substituted for names. Also, a twice-yearly draw didn't meet the public demand. A weekly lottery was what was wanted and the various regional governments were quick to see the revenue possibilities.

HISTORY OF THE LOTTERIES

1566: The lottery idea had caught the imagination of the English. The Southeast coastal towns of Hastings, Romany, Hythe, and Dover all needed costly harbour repairs. The mayor sought advice from the Warden of the Ports, who went to Queen Elizabeth I. And it was she who, as it were, set the first English lottery wheels in motion by authorising a state lottery to pay for repairs to the harbours. It was launched in 1567. There were 400,000 tickets, with a top prize of the equivalent of about £10,000.

1612: An English lottery was sanctioned by James I in 1612 and raised the equivalent of £100,000 for some American colonists.

Although most lotteries of this period were to raise funds for charities, etc. other lotteries were run for more dubious reasons and often people hesitated before buying tickets because they feared that the outcome might be fixed.

HISTORY OF THE LOTTERIES

Louis XIV of France drew the tickets for a lottery in the 17th century and landed a 100,000-Franc prize for himself and smaller prizes for the Queen and the Dauphin. The people's anger was stilled only when the King graciously handed the money back and requested that it be drawn for again.

One thing was evident - whether they were honest or crooked, philanthropic or profiteering, lotteries offered a reliable source of income.
Hard-pressed governments couldn't ignore this fact for long, and so state-run lotteries gradually began to make their appearance throughout Europe.

1700: In Britain, lotteries have had a rough passage. "Lotteries exist to the utter ruin and impoverishment of many families and to the reproach of the English laws and government," says a law prohibiting lotteries that appeared in 1700, toward the end of the reign of William III - who had himself been fighting his Augsburg battles on the income from a lottery. Throughout the succeeding centuries, different British governments had different ideas about lotteries, some allowing them, some outlawing them.

HISTORY OF THE LOTTERIES

1956: Britain's government-run lottery was introduced and was totally unlike the various state lotteries in Europe. It is commonly called "Premium Bonds", and is in effect a form of investing money in the state. The bonds themselves can be bought for £1 each at post offices and banks. Three months after their purchase, bonds become eligible for the monthly draw. Bond numbers are selected by an electronic machine known as "Ernie" (Electronic Random Number Indicator Equipment). and tax free prizes from the equivalent of £50 to £10,000 are won by the holders of drawn numbers.

1994: The British Governments reinstates the National Lottery. Britain may be the last country in Europe to run the National Lottery but it promises to be the most spectacular in the world.

PAST & PRESENT LOTTERY TICKETS

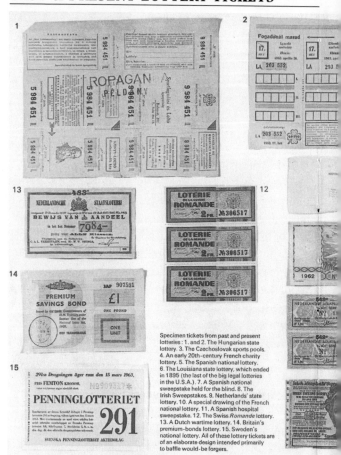

Specimen tickets from past and present lotteries: 1. and 2. The Hungarian state lottery. 3. The Czechoslovak sports pools. 4. An early 20th-century French charity lottery. 5. The Spanish national lottery. 6. The Louisiana state lottery, which ended in 1895 (the last of the big legal lotteries in the U.S.A.). 7. A Spanish national sweepstake held for the blind. 8. The Irish Sweepstakes. 9. Netherlands' state lottery. 10. A special drawing of the French national lottery. 11. A Spanish hospital sweepstake. 12. The Swiss *Romande* lottery. 13. A Dutch wartime lottery. 14. Britain's premium-bonds lottery. 15. Sweden's national lottery. All of these lottery tickets are of an elaborate design intended primarily to baffle would-be forgers.

PAST & PRESENT LOTTERY TICKETS

LOTTERIES AROUND THE WORLD

There are over 170 lotteries around the world with sales totalling over £60 billion per year - that is almost the same as the annual salary of U.K's total workforce.

SPAIN: Whose lottery Loteria Nacional is one of the largest in the world, originated in 1811 at which time it was called Loteria Moderna. Until 1892 it co-existed with Loteria Primitiva, a lottery which started in 1763 established by the Ministry of Treasury during the reign of Carlos III.

Tickets for the Loteria Nacional can be obtained in 4000 ticket offices located all over Spain. The price of the tickets varies according to the quantity of numbers you wish to buy. A set of numbers costs 30,000 pesetas and the minimum amount to be bought is ten which costs 3000 Pesetas.

ITALY: There is at least one lottery office in every Italian town . Each office is under the control of a manager who runs it as an individual business.   In each of the 3500 registered lottery offices a draw is held weekly from tickets bearing the numbers 1 - 90. Five numbers are drawn.

LOTTERIES AROUND THE WORLD

FRANCE: The French take their lottery very seriously. Few streets in Paris lack their little booths set up on corners, under cafe awnings, or other approachable places. The state controlled lotteries in France have weekly draws as well as special draws at Christmas, Easter, etc., and other chosen occasions when the prizes are increased enormously.

GERMANY: There are two main lotteries in Germany, the North West German lottery Nordwestdeutsche Klassen-lotterie and the southern part lottery Suddeutsche Klassen-lotterie. The lotteries are run under the supervision of the governments of the above-named Federal States who are responsible for their activities.

U.S.A.: Until recently no legal lottery existed in the USA except in the dependency of Puerto Rico. But in April 1963 the Governor of New Hampshire authorised a state lottery which he hoped would raise $4,000,000 a year for state education. But this is not to say that lotteries didn't flourish illegally elsewhere in America Today lotteries are big business in America with a separate lottery for each individual state.

HOW THE NATIONAL LOTTERY WILL WORK.

The National Lottery is expected to be a big hit with a British public dreaming of becoming millionaires overnight - it will be the world's largest computerised lottery, with prizes ranging from £5 up to £1,000,000.

40,000,000 tickets a week will be sold at up to 30,000 retail outlets nation-wide. Primarily an impulse buy, they will be available wherever one might be expected to carry loose change - at newsagents, petrol stations, high street shops, convenience stores and shopping centres. The procedure is simple. The customer buys a ticket at the retail agent and selects six numbers or if preferred, the local computer terminal will select them at random.

The terminal communicates the selected numbers to a central computer where the information is read and a security number generated. The verified ticket is then transmitted back to the local terminal which issues the completed lottery ticket displaying the chosen numbers and security date. The entire operation should take less than five seconds.

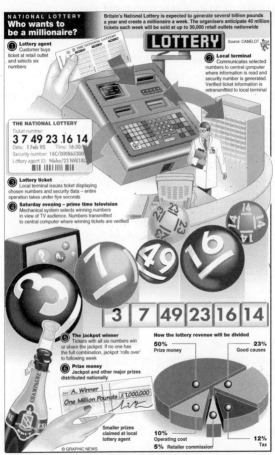

NATIONAL LOTTERY
Who wants to be a millionaire?

Britain's National Lottery is expected to generate several billion pounds a year and create a millionaire a week. The organisers anticipate 40 million tickets each week will be sold at up to 30,000 retail outlets nationwide

Source: CAMELOT

① Lottery agent
Customer buys ticket at retail outlet and selects six numbers

② Local terminal
Communicates selected numbers to central computer where information is read and security number is generated. Verified ticket information is retransmitted to local terminal

THE NATIONAL LOTTERY
Ticket number:
3 7 49 23 16 14
Date: 1 Feb 95   Time: 16:30s
Security number: 16C/000865300
Lottery agent ID: Nisha/23 NW18L

③ Lottery ticket
Local terminal issues ticket displaying chosen numbers and security data – entire operation takes under five seconds

④ Saturday evening – prime time television
Mechanical system selects winning numbers in view of TV audience. Numbers transmitted to central computer where winning tickets are verified

3 7 49 23 16 14

⑤ The jackpot winner
Tickets with all six numbers win or share the jackpot. If no one has the full combination, jackpot 'rolls over' to following week

⑥ Prize money
Jackpot and other major prizes distributed nationally

PAY A. Winner
One Million Pounds £1,000,000

Smaller prizes claimed at local lottery agent

How the lottery revenue will be divided
- 50% Prize money
- 23% Good causes
- 12% Tax
- 5% Retailer commission
- 10% Operating cost

© GRAPHIC NEWS

GRAPHIC NEWS

Utopia Village, 7 Chalcot Road, London NW1 8LH, United Kingdom.
Tel: +44 71 722 4673. Fax: +44 71 586 3567

WHERE WILL THE MONEY GO?

A new millionaire will be revealed each Saturday evening on prime-time television . A mechanical system, such as numbered balls falling at random, selects the winning numbers in view of the TV audience and the numbers are transmitted to the central computer for verification. Anyone with all six numbers wins the jackpot - if no one has the full combination the jackpot 'rolls over' to the following week, increasing the prize money

The winners of prizes of up to £50 can claim their winnings at their local lottery agent while larger prizes will be distributed at regional centres.

Lottery revenue is estimated at £3 billion a year within three years of its launch. 50 percent will be distributed in prize money while 23 percent, (about £690 million) will be divided equally between five good causes - the arts, sport, charities, National Heritage, and the Millennium fund. 12 per cent, or £360 million, will disappear in tax leaving 15 per cent - £450 million - to cover operating costs and commission for the retailer

Source: Camelot

The National Lottery will probably become the largest single "consumer product" in the UK. It will be a complex project of material importance. It will demand expertise in consumer marketing and distribution, security, lotteries, electronic data networks and computer systems. The company chosen to take on board this huge project is in an unrivalled position to provide these skills. With their pedigree of lottery experience world-wide, they are well placed to ensure the successful launch and operation of the UK National Lottery.

Camelot Group Plc is made up of the following five companies each with it's own expertise in the operation needed to run the project.

The Companies are:

Cadbury Schweppes Plc (22.5%0 is a major international company in confectionery and beverages, who is a market leader in fast moving consumer goods, with its' brands widely distributed in retail outlets throughout the UK.

Source: Camelot

De La Rue Plc (22.5%) is the world's largest high security printer, supplying bank notes to over 100 Governments. De La Rue has been involved in the lottery industry for over 20 years.

GTECH UK LTD (22.5%) is a subsidiary of GTECH Corporation, the world's leading supplier and operator of Government Lotteries. They design, install, maintain and support lottery systems for 69 states.

Racal Electronics Plc (22.5%0 is a world leading professional electronics communications company. Racal currently runs the Government Data Network linking hundreds of Government offices around the UK.

ICL (10%) is a leading information technology company specialising in systems integration in selected markets. ICL operates in 80 countries with half its' business generating software and services.

Source: Camelot

WHAT ARE THE ODDS?

The probability of an event is the number of chances favourable to that event happening compared with the total number of possible chances, so long as all the possible chances are equally likely to happen.

The odds of winning the National Lottery as worked out by our mathematician are:

Getting	6	out of	6	The odds are :	$114 \times 10^9 : 1$
Getting	5	out of	6	The odds are:	$476 \times 10^5 : 1$
Getting	4	out of	6	The odds are:	$416 \times 10^3 : 1$
Getting	3	out of	6	The odds are:	$6249 : 1$
Getting	2	out of	6	The odds are:	$1746 : 1$
Getting	1	out of	6	The odds are:	$91 : 1$

This may be explained further by the following comparisons:
The odds against obtaining the jackpot on the National Lottery are approximately the same as obtaining:

- 34 heads in 34 tosses of a fair coin
- Between 9 and 10 double 6's consecutively rolling a pair of dice.

WHAT ARE THE ODDS?

So there you have it...... The odds are not too impressive but it is only a game of chance.

COMPARISON OF THE ODDS FOR OTHER EVENTS

COIN TOSSING

1 head in 1 toss the odds are	$1 : 1$
5 heads in 5 tosses the odds are	$31 : 1$
10 heads in 10 tosses the odds are	$1023 : 1$
20 heads in 20 tosses the odds are	$1048575 : 1$
40 heads in 40 tosses the odds are	$1.1 \times 10^{12} : 1$

ROULETTE

(00 - 32) 7 successive correct numbers - the odds are 5.26×10^{10}

FOOTBALL POOLS

under 30% payout.
All 8 jackpot draws out of 54 matches - the odds are $10^9 : 1$

WHAT ARE THE ODDS?

IN POKER
The Odds of being dealt the following hands in a fair Poker Game, from one pack of cards are...

Royal Flush	1 in	649,740
Straight Flush	1 in	72,193
Four of a Kind	1 in	4,165
Full House	1 in	694
Flush	1 in	509
Three of a Kind	1 in	47
One Pair	1 in	2

DICE THROWING
In throwing a single dice, there are six possible cases. You therefore, have a 1 in 5 chance of throwing a specific number in one throw. The odds are 5 to 1.

With a pair of dice:
- getting any double   35 to 1
- getting a total of 11   17 to 1
- getting a total of 7   5 to 1

WHY DO PEOPLE GAMBLE?

Why do people gamble? What is it that makes the placing of a bet and the awaiting of its outcome so very exciting? It isn't easy to answer these questions. What is possible however, is to analyse the psychological behaviour of man and list a number of motives which may or may not relate to any particular gambler.

People therefore gamble for the following reasons:

1:   The acquisition of unearned money, i.e. a form of greed.

2:   Social cachet (snobbery),

3:   Sexual compensation,

4.   Masochism,

5:   Boredom,

6:   Intellectual exercise,

7:   The desire to prove one's superiority to the forces of chance, or

8:   Inexplicable excitement.

Or any combination of the above

WHY DO PEOPLE GAMBLE?

These motives were devised by Alan Wykes in his book "Gambling". Mr Wykes singled out 128 serious gamblers - all known to him personally - to whom he sent a questionnaire and invited the recipients to indicate any that they felt might apply to others if not themselves.

A quick look through the replies to the suggestionnaire showed that only reasons 6 and 8 would be seen by the recipients as applicable to themselves. Reasons 1 (greed) and 2 (snobbery) were attributed to gamblers other than the recipients. Reasons 3 (sexual compensation) and 4 (masochism) got me nothing g but some unprintable ribald comments. And only a very few respondents even bothered to consider 5 (boredom) or 7 (the desire to prove one's superiority to the forces of chance).

Whatever motive a gambler may have; you can be certain that he or she will never honestly admit to it - not just to others, but even to themselves.

If you are one of those who never wins anything don't give in too easily, you may not have been lucky up until now but you will never win anything if you don't enter. It is no good going around moaning that you never win the Lottery unless you invest in a ticket!! Enter everything, is my advice and the odds are eventually you will win something.

Apart from working for it, there are three main ways to get your hands on big money. You can either steal it or inherit it or win it.

Stealing isn't a good idea. There was a case recently of two guys who attempted to hold up a Building Society, they were equipped with sawn off shotguns but made the mistake of wearing a pair of tights over their heads, unfortunately they forgot to cut the crotch, therefore it did not make for a smooth get-away when they attempted to leave by different exits.

Inheriting is all very well, but this means that you must know somebody who is very rich and likes you enough to leave you their money.

So the other alternative way is to win it, and remember you are only six numbers away from that jackpot prize.

THE ADVANTAGES OF WINNING

Think about the advantages of winning large amounts of money. For a start it is going to make you an awful lot more attractive to the opposite sex. Right now you might be a short, fat, balding little Herbert with acne and halitosis that repels green fly at twenty paces. However, if you were all of the above and rich too it wouldn't matter, you would be absolutely guaranteed to score. For example, we all know the story of the guy who approached a woman at a party and asked her if she would sleep with him for a million pounds "Of course" she replied without hesitation. "Well, OK." he said, "Would you sleep with me for two pounds?" at this juncture she slapped his face "What sort of girl do you thin I am" she spluttered, "We've already established that" he said "Now we're merely bartering over the price".

You will also find that you never again have to queue for tables in the best restaurants. That supercilious little head waiter that used to look at you as though you were something unpleasant on the bottom of his shoe is ushering you to the best table and offering you champagne on the house. Don't be fooled, he still doesn't like you, he's just hoping for a large tip.

GIVING UP YOUR DAY JOB

You may have read stories of people who have won colossal amounts of money who say silly things like "I won't give be giving up my job at the Abattoir", take no notice of this sort of wild talk, it is merely attributable to shock. Once they wake up they'll soon be off down to book a year in the Bahamas. For those who do actually mean it, I would just like to extend to them my deepest sympathy and pass on this piece of advice GET A LIFE!!!! For most of us the chance to tell your Boss where to stick his job is just too good an opportunity to miss.

> *"You're late, you have been warned,*
> *and that's the fourth day in a row*
> *I don't pay you to just stroll in*
> *at any time you know*
> *You've got a lot of work to do*
> *I won't let you mess about*
> *and if you turn up late again*
> *I'm telling you you're out"*
> *You say "I'm really sorry Sir"*
> *if it's drive that I have lacked*
> *but now I'm rich*
> *I've bought the Company*
> *and as for you YOU'RE SACKED.*

A WARM UP EXERCISE IN GETTING STARTED

Before we get started dealing with the intricacies of The National Lottery and ways in which you can win, it may be worth indulging in a warm-up exercise which will help to demonstrate in a clear unscientific way your chances of winning the jackpot in the National Lottery.

The idea is to pinpoint anyone of the dots on the opposite page, hang the book on the wall, move back ten feet, and try hitting the spot dead on with a broken old dart, whilst blindfolded.

A formidable task? .... Maybe, but you will never know unless you try, and perhaps once you have read through this book, your perception will change and you may become less rational, and even more equipped to play the game. Remember, even if you don't win the National Lottery, you always have the following words to turn to for comfort.

For when the one Great Scorer
Comes to mark against your name
He writes - not that you have won or lost
but how you played the game.

A WARM UP EXERCISE

HOW TO WIN THE LOTTERY

Let's explore the possibilities, how indeed are you going to get this magical sum? Well, there's a good chance you could win either by fair means or foul, which all depends on your principles.

A Canadian woman has won the National Lottery a record 3 times - how is this possible you ask yourself? - well, actually she's sleeping with the guy who programmes the computer. You could try it but it won't work for everyone.

The other alternative is to forgave the winning ticket - OK there is always a chance you could be found out and sent down for along time. The up side of this is that when you come out you will have at least learnt something. Yes that's right - by then your forgeries will be really convincing!!!!!

Or you come across somebody who as already the winning ticket, just for instance you may come across a drunk lying face down in the gutter with the winning ticket sticking you of his back pocket - what would you do??? YES!! you and I both know exactly what you'd do, so just a tip, if you ever are lucky enough t win, don't get drunk until AFTER you have collected the winnings!!

THE MOST DESPERATE MEANS

There are also those real nutters who are so determined to win, that they go to any lengths.

HOW TO PICK THE WINNING NUMBERS

There are people who claim they can predict the winning numbers. For instance visiting fortune tellers is a very popular way of discovering whether or not your luck is about to change. But when she tells you that she can

see large amounts of money changing hands, don't be too taken in – the money in question will be passing from your hands to hers.

Then of course there are the real eccentrics (nutters!!) who claim that they let their pets pick their winning numbers for them.

While you are waiting for your pet or whoever to pick the winning numbers for you; here's a few one liners to past the time....

What do you call a guy that wins the Lottery and the Pools in the same week?
A LUCKY BASTARD!!!!

What do you call your neighbour who has just won the Lottery?
MATE!!!!!

What do you call a 7 foot psychopath who has just won the Lottery?
SIR!!

If you don't have any luck winning the lottery yourself, then try to share in someone else's good fortune - you could try putting an ad in the lonely hearts column;

"18 year old curvy sex kitten seeks lottery winner for erotic weekends, age and looks not important."

HOW TO PICK THE WINNING NUMBERS

Whatever means you use to pick those lottery winning numbers, just be patient with those who are trying so hard to pick them for you.

THE HIDDEN WINNING LOTTERY NUMBERS

This photograph is designed for those of who wish to choose you six lottery numbers with a little bit of effort, so that on winning the jackpot you can claim to have worked the numbers out instead of just picking them from the air or having someone else pick them for you.

All you have to do is to work out the answers to the following questions, put the answers to the six questions which relate to each other best together; and who knows? - you may have the winning numbers.

How many people are wearing long sleeves?
How many people are wearing hats?
How many people are drinking?
How many people are wearing glasses?
How many people are smoking?
How many people are wearing ties?
How many people are talking?
How many people are smiling?
How many people are looking bored?
How many people are showing their legs?
How many people are biting their nails?
How many people are wearing watches?
How many people are with children?
How many people are picking their nose?

PICTURE WITH THE HIDDEN
WINNING NUMBERS

NO SUCH LUCK

There are those who are just not meant to win - regardless of whether their numbers come up or not. A good example of a guy who had used his wife's vital statistics for his winning ticket for years diligently using 42 33 40 every week for twenty years until the day his wife discovered diet and exercise, thereby changing her shape and his numbers. He loyally changed his numbers to his wife's new statistics on the week that the original numbers came up.

A compulsive gambler eventually won the big one on the lottery and thought he would double his money so he put it all on a horse - yes, you know what happened next don't you-you're wrong he won!! It was the horse he put it on after that, that fell at the first fence.

Another guy from Connecticut received the news that he had won a share of 4 million dollars in the state lottery - the actual amount to be revealed on the day. Full of excitement he hired a plane and had his whole family flown down in style to the award ceremony only to discover that the computer had blipped that week and there were in actual fact 4 million winners - yep that's right he had won a dollar!!!

IT'S JUST NOT MEANT TO BE

Then there's the other instances of the poor people who do the lottery, check the lottery and find they've won the lottery only to discover that they have lost the ticket!!!

Or the very sad case of the man who opened his mail to find a cheque from the Lottery company. He glanced at the signature, waltzed his wife round the kitchen, leapt into hi car and drove to work. He stormed past his bosses' secretary and told his boss to stick his job where the sun don't shine. His old boss smiled benignly at him as he accepted his resignation. The guy was just on his way out of the office when the boss stopped him "Oh by the way, your wife phoned, you misread the cheque - it was actually for the bloke next door!!"

Or the guy in New York who saw his winning number in the New York Gazette, he rushed home and looked everywhere for his ticket then remembered that he had put it into the pocket of his suit which was now at the cleaners. He rushed down there to retrieve it only to find a note on the door which read "Gone to the Caribbean - Closed indefinitely"!!!!

DEAD RICH

There are of course those unfortunate people for whom the shock of winning could prove to be the final straw ......

From the other point of view there are those wives who are convinced they have got their just desserts if their other half keels over at the news. He has probably been unfaithful for years, and now she is rich, she has the means to buy him a really elaborate headstone.
but what should she put on it...........

> *If I could only see you smile*
> *to sit down and just talk awhile*
> *I'd like to ask you, you old toad*
> *what you saw in Glady's down the road*
> *it wasn't worship from afar*
> *'cause I found her knickers in our car*
> *now you are gone and I am rich*
> *and in prison – 'cause I shot the bitch*

Then there's the story of the Spanish Guy had a rich Uncle who had no other living relatives. The nephew knew that the old guy had recently won the lottery but had not yet cashed in his ticket.

Therefore he would visit him everyday and bath him, cut his toe-nails etc. Eventually after many patient years waiting by the nephew the old guy died. He visited the Solicitor and waited with baited breath for the news. The Solicitor handed over the coveted lottery ticket to the nephew saying "That's the good news" "The bad news is the expiry date on the claim was yesterday!!!"

Sometimes despite your numerous attempts you find that may be you were just never meant to win, but then as a surprise consultation you find that a loved one in the family has won instead.

You must consider this as a blessing, because you will not need to go through sleepless nights and the worry of having all that money to yourself; unless of course that loved one suddenly accidentally passes away. In which case remember to honour her/his memory and choose the words on the tombstone carefully.

BE HAPPY FOR THE WINNER

THE DISADVANTAGES OF WINNING

An extra drawback might be that people who haven't spoken to you for years may suddenly crave your company and extend invitations to meals and the like. Nip this one firmly in the bud as soon as possible.

The other problem with owning this sort of money is the tiresome begging letters, but as nay Lottery winner worth their weight will tell you, it pays to keep sending them.

For instance a guy in Chicago won 2.6 million dollars on the lottery and having been brought up in a very poor family and always being short of food, the money went to his head. He'd heard that the rich were also eccentric, so he decided that he would follow that mode. For three years he lived entirely on doughnuts - never leaving his penthouse apartment and never washing or changing his clothes, friends visited and were appaled at the amount of weight he had gained through his unhealthy diet. He eventually died at the age of 28 from strangulation - was he murdered for his money ? well not actually, the collar on his short just got too tight and choked him.!

DREAMS COME TRUE

Not all of these stories are sad though, there have been
occasions when people really have come up the big one
and they have spent their money in ways that they have
always dreamed............

DOING IT IN STYLE

If you are lucky enough to come into the sort of money which means that you get to rub shoulders with the rich and famous, it is essential to conduct yourself with a little finesse if you want to fit in. For instance here are 10 things you should never do when staying at the Carlton in Cannes....

Ask how much the rooms are
Pinch the receptionists bottom
Wash your feet in the bidet
Demand ketchup with your caviar
Order Steak Tartare well done
Wipe your nose on the table-cloth
Call the Maitre'd
Nick the towels
Compare it to Majorca.....And finally....
When room service intimate that a small tip may be on the agenda do NOT advise them to "Wash their whites separately"! !

The best advice is to study the Rich, by this I mean the real Rich, the ones that have always had money, not just come upon it by sheer good fortune - there is nothing wrong with being newly rich, the secret is not to look it!

MONEY TALKS

The most astonishing thing that you will find about winning the Lottery is that the more money you have the less you will need. People who up until now could hardly force themselves to give you the time of day will be falling over themselves to buy you meals and drinks. One profession that particularly falls into this category is your Bank Manager. In the past, you may find that the only contact you have had with this character has been in the form of sarcastic and threatening letters advising you to settle your outstanding overdraft lest he be forced to cancel your credit facilities. If anyone is going to do any crawling from now on it sure as hell won't be you

Ah, Good morning Richards.
Oh, you haven't got much time?
No it's not about my overdraft,
as far as that's concerned I'm fine.
So you think that is a problem?
Well I don't mean to be funny,
I can tell you haven't heard yet
but I've won a lot of money
Oh ,Its just over a million
yeah !or close to that amount.
No I don't want Tea, don't crawl to me
I'm closing my account.

MONEY CAN BUY REVENGE

With money, you can indulge in your wildest fantasy even if it is getting your own back.

SHARED WEALTH

There are other people who are entirely selfless with their money and will spend it on giving pleasure to others ....

SHARED WEALTH

And yet others who are prepared to spend their hard won cash on buying back treasured possessions that their Country has inadvertently or carelessly lost.

KEEPING UP APPEARANCES

People who have had money in the family for generations always dress down. So if you want to be accepted as one of the 'Country Set' a head scarf, old tweed skirt and green wellies are the order of the day.

KEEPING UP APPEARANCES

You may wish to move to a better neighbourhood, and when you do, remember to behave in a manner befitting your new financial status.

Once the stone cladding is finished, it should look a treat..

WHAT WOULD I DO WITH ALL THAT MONEY?

In actual fact, in the right hands, this kind of money could change your whole existence. No longer would you have to worry about your appearance or the fact that you were overweight- with money you could be anything you want! You could have a face lift, a hair transplant, liposuctiion - the list is endless.

I'm going to get my nose done
I'm going to buy nice things
I'm after all those trappings
that only money brings
'Cause I have won the lottery
I've had a change of luck
I'll go out nights, I'll buy new tights
I'll live like lady muck
I'll hire a load of servants
I'm so rich it's obscene
and when the plastic surgeons finished
I'll look just like the Queen
Then I'll divorce my husband
I never liked the louse
I'll have some fun and when that's done
I'll buy my council house!!!!!

BUYING YOUR FIRST HOME

Of course some people have ambitions that are a little more extravagant

A FOOL AND HIS MONEY

Now you are a millionaire you must get used to the idea that every pimply-faced little entrepreneur in the vicinity is going to approach you to finance their latest hare-brained scheme. Although it is probably a good idea to invest your money in something, be sensible about it and don't sink it into the very first scheme that comes along.

I had some money to invest
In truth five hundred grand
I searched for good inventors
up and down the land
I wanted something different
a thing not seen before
I wanted to be richer
and famous what is more
So I met this bloke who told me
he could make my dreams come true
he showed me round his prototype
and I believed him too
He said I'd be a household name
that he would keep my name alive
and I'm the berk who lost his money
in the great Sinclair C5.

A FOOL AND HIS MONEY

Did you hear about the Irish guy who won the Lottery?
He lit his cigar with the ticket to celebrate!

LESS GENEROUS WINNERS

A Scotsman on hearing that he was about to be the recipient of a million pounds agreed to come to the awards ceremony only if the presenters paid his return train fare and put him up overnight. When challenged he said "Well if they can afford to give away a million quid they've got more money than I have !!!

LESS GENEROUS WINNERS

It's not only the Scots who are careful with their money, many of their English counterparts, on suddenly receiving large unexpected sums of money, suddenly become very mistrustful and are very wary of letting other people near their cash.

AND FINALLY; IF YOU HAVEN'T WON

A sure fire way of increasing your chances of winning the lottery is to buy lots of tickets.

CHARITY BEGINS AT HOME

Having got all this cash, it would be fairly selfish of you to keep it all to yourself, so perhaps it would be a nice idea to make a few small donations to deserving charities.

KEEP TRACK OF YOUR NUMBERS

DRAW DATE	LOTTERY NUMBERS BOUGHT	LOTTERY NUMBERS DRAWN
	—,—,—,—,—,—	—,—,—,—,—,—
	—,—,—,—,—,—	—,—,—,—,—,—
	—,—,—,—,—,—	—,—,—,—,—,—
	—,—,—,—,—,—	—,—,—,—,—,—
	—,—,—,—,—,—	—,—,—,—,—,—
	—,—,—,—,—,—	—,—,—,—,—,—
	—,—,—,—,—,—	—,—,—,—,—,—
	—,—,—,—,—,—	—,—,—,—,—,—
	—,—,—,—,—,—	—,—,—,—,—,—
	—,—,—,—,—,—	—,—,—,—,—,—
	—,—,—,—,—,—	—,—,—,—,—,—
	—,—,—,—,—,—	—,—,—,—,—,—

KEEP TRACK OF YOUR NUMBERS

LOTTERY NUMBERS MATCHED	AMOUNT WON	LIST OF LUCKY NUMBERS
—,—,—,—,—,—,	£	—,—,—,—,—,—,
—,—,—,—,—,—,	£	—,—,—,—,—,—,
—,—,—,—,—,—,	£	—,—,—,—,—,—,
—,—,—,—,—,—,	£	—,—,—,—,—,—,
—,—,—,—,—,—,	£	—,—,—,—,—,—,
—,—,—,—,—,—,	£	—,—,—,—,—,—,
—,—,—,—,—,—,	£	—,—,—,—,—,—,
—,—,—,—,—,—,	£	—,—,—,—,—,—,
—,—,—,—,—,—,	£	—,—,—,—,—,—,
—,—,—,—,—,—,	£	—,—,—,—,—,—,
—,—,—,—,—,—,	£	—,—,—,—,—,—,
—,—,—,—,—,—,	£	—,—,—,—,—,—,

KEEP TRACK OF YOUR NUMBERS

DRAW DATE	LOTTERY NUMBERS BOUGHT	LOTTERY NUMBERS DRAWN
	—,—,—,—,—,—,	—,—,—,—,—,—,
	—,—,—,—,—,—,	—,—,—,—,—,—,
	—,—,—,—,—,—,	—,—,—,—,—,—,
	—,—,—,—,—,—,	—,—,—,—,—,—,
	—,—,—,—,—,—,	—,—,—,—,—,—,
	—,—,—,—,—,—,	—,—,—,—,—,—,
	—,—,—,—,—,—,	—,—,—,—,—,—,
	—,—,—,—,—,—,	—,—,—,—,—,—,
	—,—,—,—,—,—,	—,—,—,—,—,—,
	—,—,—,—,—,—,	—,—,—,—,—,—,
	—,—,—,—,—,—,	—,—,—,—,—,—,
	—,—,—,—,—,—,	—,—,—,—,—,—,

KEEP TRACK OF YOUR NUMBERS

LOTTERY NUMBERS MATCHED	AMOUNT WON	LIST OF LUCKY NUMBERS
—,—,—,—,—,	£	—,—,—,—,—,
—,—,—,—,—,	£	—,—,—,—,—,
—,—,—,—,—,	£	—,—,—,—,—,
—,—,—,—,—,	£	—,—,—,—,—,
—,—,—,—,—,	£	—,—,—,—,—,
—,—,—,—,—,	£	—,—,—,—,—,
—,—,—,—,—,	£	—,—,—,—,—,
—,—,—,—,—,	£	—,—,—,—,—,
—,—,—,—,—,	£	—,—,—,—,—,
—,—,—,—,—,	£	—,—,—,—,—,
—,—,—,—,—,	£	—,—,—,—,—,

LIST OF YOUR LOCAL AGENTS

Name of Agent: ....

Address of Agent: ....

....

....

Telephone number: ....

Opening hours: ....

Agency number: ....

Name of Agent: ....

Address of Agent: ....

....

....

Telephone number: ....

Opening hours: ....

Agency number: ....

LIST OF YOUR LOCAL AGENTS

Name of Agent: ....

Address of Agent: ....

....

....

Telephone number: ....

Opening hours: ....

Agency number: ....

Name of Agent: ....

Address of Agent: ....

....

....

Telephone number: ....

Opening hours: ....

Agency number: ....

MONIES INVESTED

DRAW DATE	MONEY INVESTED	MONEY WON	BALANCE
	£......................	£......................	£......................
	£......................	£......................	£......................
	£......................	£......................	£......................
	£......................	£......................	£......................
	£......................	£......................	£......................
	£......................	£......................	£......................
	£......................	£......................	£......................
	£......................	£......................	£......................
	£......................	£......................	£......................
	£......................	£......................	£......................
	£......................	£......................	£......................
	£......................	£......................	£......................

LIST OF CREDITS FOR ILLUSTRATIONS/ WORKS/QUOTES ETC

The book "Gambling" by Alan Wykes, by kind permission of Mrs M. Wykes.
Illustrations on pages: 14, 15, 43
Extracts adapted on pages: 8 - 13, 17, 25-27.

Graphic News: 18, 19.
Under licence from Graphic News.

Camelot Press Information: 20, 21, 22.

Our compliments to:

Standard Press Analysts.   Tel: 071 403 7413

We are entering the age of the "information enter-prise". It is increasingly acknowledged that the businesses that will emerge as successful in this changing environment are those that most effec-tively make use of the information available to them. Enabling organisations to detect and respond to market trends, to pre-empt competitive threats, and to develop successful new initiatives.

Standard Press Analysts offer an intelligent, per-ceptive and hot-off-the-presses monitoring service covering a carefully selected range of influential UK and US publications.

LIST OF TITLES FROM
IDEAS UNLIMITED (PUBLISHING)

Please send me (Postage free UK):

copies "100 CHAT UP LINES"
ISBN: 1 871964 00 8 (128 pages A7) @ £1.99

copies "THE IDIOTS HANDBOOK OF LOVE & SEX"
ISBN: 1 871964 08 3 (128 pages A7) @ £1.99

copies "10 GOLDEN RULES OF CHATTING UP"
ISBN: 1 871964 09 1 (128 pages A7) @ £1.99

copies "SIZE ISN'T EVERYTHING"
ISBN: 1 871964 12 1 (64 pages A7) @ £1.99

copies "OF COURSE I LOVE YOU"
ISBN: 1 871964 01 6 (96 pages A6) @ £1.99

copies "WELL HUNG"
ISBN: 1 871964 07 5 (96 pages A5) @ £2.99

copies "BODY LANGUAGE SEX SIGNALS"
ISBN: 1 871964 06 7 (64 pages) @ £2.50

copies "BEGINNERS GUIDE TO KISSING"
ISBN: 1 871964 02 4 (64 pages A5) @ £2.50

copies "TIPS FOR A SUCCESSFUL MARRIAGE"
ISBN: 1 871964 03 2 (64 pages A5) @ £2.50

copies "JOY OF FATHERHOOD"
ISBN: 1 871964 04 0 (64 pages A5) @ £2.50

copies "OFFICE HANKY PANKY"
ISBN: 1 871964 05 9 (64 pages A5) @ £2.50

copies "SPORT FOR THE ELDERLY"
ISBN: 1 871964 11 3 (48 pages A5) @ £2.50

copies "HAVE YOU SEEN THE NOTICE BOARD?"
ISBN: 1 871964 10 5 (80 pages A4) @ £3.99

copies "HOW TO WIN THE NATIONAL LOTTERY"
ISBN: 1 871964 14 8 (80 pages A7) @ £1.99

I have enclosed a cheque/postal order for £ ....
made payable to IDEAS UNLIMITED (PUBLISHING)

NAME: ....

ADDRESS: ....

....

....

....

COUNTY: .... POST CODE: ....

Fill in the coupon above and send it with your payment to:

IDEAS UNLIMITED (PUBLISHING)
PO BOX 125
PORTSMOUTH
HAMPSHIRE
PO1 4PP

Postage free within the UK.

If you wish your purchase to be sent directly to someone else
(eg, Birthday, Christmas, Wedding, Valentines Gift), simply fill
in their name and address in the coupon above and enclose
your cheque/postal order with your personal message or card,
if desired. We will be pleased to send your gift directly to your
chosen recipient.